Contents

Introduction

I write this guide as an educational resource exclusively. It is MY attempt at earning legitimate money using information I've acquired and interpreted for you, the average Joe (or Joanne). I do NOT condone criminal acts. I've been the victim of such acts before. It sucks. Should you decide to proceed with nefarious activity, I only ask that you play Robin Hood and donate something to the many other desperate people in this world. Who and how is up to you, as you well know. Accumulated acts of kindness might have prevented your real curiosity in reading this guide, so if you must hurt someone, then please try to make the world at least a slightly better place as penance.

THIS INFORMATION IS LEGAL TO POSSESS IN THE US AND IS PROTECTED BY THE UNITED STATES' FIRST AMENDMENT RIGHT TO FREE SPEECH.

Having stated the previous paragraph, use this information at your own peril, because law enforcement MAY use your possession of this information as evidence of conspiracy if they have other evidence of you being naughty. Be careful and don't have your lawyers contact me if you get locked up. Just read this for entertainment purposes and to illustrate the ease of identity and other online theft. This book should scare you, or at least make you a little nervous.

Most techies guard their knowledge jealously. They are afraid to reveal what they know out of fear they will be replaced. I'm getting old. There are far more days behind me than ahead, so sharing my intuitive ability to translate tech to English is a kind of parting gift. How you use it is up to you. This world could be a much better place if the people in authority didn't abuse their power. Sadly, we humans are born with the curses of greed and pride.

Put these things behind you, and use this book to force those unwilling to play nice, to play by the rules. Don't let others' bad behavior, influence yours. Of all else, though, choose a path and lead.

1: **Fraud**

I begin this guide with fraud. The statistics on fraud are amazing[1]. Everyone has either been a victim or knows somebody who has been. In fact, these days it's more likely that most everyone with any type of credit has been targeted (or is *currently* being attacked) without their knowledge. They may never even find out – ever!

Fraud is so common today that we commit it without even blinking an eye. Use your wife's credit card, write an unfunded check, fudge on your taxes. Akin to traveling a few mph over the speed limit, we've become numb to it and most offenses go unpunished or even recognized. Our society has SO many laws,

---

1   www.statisticbrain.com/identity-theft-fraud-statistics/

rules, and regulations that we've developed a general disdain towards them, even contempt. Violations have become routine, and punishment a cost of living.

The Internet has enabled a vast number of people to attack your finances and identity at will. Entire marketplaces have been erected and are booming based on these dastardly efforts. The basic motivation is greed and the all-too-human desire for attention. You can't beat them. Law enforcement, financial institutions, software security companies, all invest huge resources into your protection and prevention, to little avail. This is an impossible battle, like a beach against the erosion from the ocean's waves.

Criminals find weaknesses. Even white hats (such as myself) look for them, constantly testing our adversaries. When the big guys are slow, we become small and nimble. Where they have countless ranks, we have anonymity. Where they have endless finances, we eliminate our expenses.

Software is a solution to a problem. Problems, however, are rarely defined clearly. So, the software solution is almost always flawed. A common misconception is the notion of perfect software. There's no such thing. The cycle of software development involves a "good enough" benchmark, then the constant resolution of bugs. It is these bugs that hackers explore and massage.

Another facet of industry is standard procedure. We call them "standard" merely because everyone else does it. Paradigm shifts aren't truly groundbreaking, they're just rewinding to an earlier mindset (before the word "standard" was attached to the concept), and exploring a different fork. It doesn't happen enough. We are a society of rushed decisions and failed reexamination. As Patton once said, "A good decision today, violently executed, is far and away better than a perfect plan tomorrow."

The financial industry, as part of their standard procedure, is creating and maintaining sub-par software vulnerable to criminals for attack. This has been going on since computers went online. The government has created entire agencies around data protection which now account for a substantial amount of our national budget. More rules, more laws, all designed to save the public from themselves.

Meanwhile, it does little good. My mother used to say, "Locks only keep honest people out," and I've found that to be a certain truism in this world. If someone wants to get in badly enough, they will. And they do. These intrusions are largely covered up, and we're just talking about hacking attacks. A single dishonest cashier or well-placed card reader can accumulate a hundred credit card numbers per day. Nobody wants to throw a monkey wrench into the system by screaming about its vulnerabilities.

The future does not bode well. There are too few competent

software programmers, and that isn't improving. The current software in-place is bloated, unreadable, and buggy. That too isn't improving. Big corporations are getting bigger, which means slower, which means they're more exposed to hacking, and fewer paradigm shifts.

This is the state of the world, like it or not. We need to expose vulnerabilities and after "they've" lost enough money, they'll fix these gaping holes. They are in a perpetual state of management by crisis, and only through crisis will they throw resources. I enjoy making people work for their money; it's not only appropriate but ideal for developing one's character.

Personal vigilance is essential and can confound the most determined attacker. By securing and changing your passwords regularly, staying abreast of your account transactions, and carefully guarding your data, you can thwart many attacks. You can't prevent them all, however, and careful monitoring is exhausting.

Someone can always steal your identity from online sources, and under current US law, you are unlikely to be notified. You can only do so much, and the rest is up to your choices in financial matters. From the DOJ website describing identity theft, "Many people do not realize how easily criminals can obtain our personal data without having to break into our homes."[2]

---

2   www.justice.gov/criminal-fraud/identity-theft/identity-theft-and-identity-fraud

2: <u>**Privacy**</u>

There is a critical misunderstanding about government agencies' abilities within the US. The general belief is that law enforcement and intelligence agencies are constitutionally prohibited from spying on you. This theory is incorrect.

They CAN and DO spy on you, but they are constitutionally prohibited from using the information gathered from spying on you, against you, in court or otherwise unless a warrant has been properly granted. That lulls most US citizens into a false sense of security. The information they gather may not be used against you NOW, but the future is always uncertain. The cases they build using the information they gather may also eventually lead to a warrant

11

Chapter 2: Privacy

legalizing future interception.

Americans hold their privacy as a cherished right, but as technology encroaches upon every facet of our existence, our actual privacy is slowly but steadily being eroded. Centuries ago, a man could have a conversation with another without legitimate fear of interception. This was the nature of the world when our constitution was drafted, and our forefathers glimpsed the possibility that this right might be compromised.

The fear was the misuse of this information - that a powerful government (unlike the one those days) could destroy the peoples' ability to control their government. The experiment of democracy hinged upon the ability of the people to overthrow a corrupt institution, and conspiracy was a necessary element of that insurrection.

Is it possible, these days, to overthrow the US government from within? Of course not. The republic has become too large to fail, like Rome, and could not recover gracefully from a correction. So, we are doomed to this plutocracy and social ills it implies. Without wealth, we are powerless, and even with some wealth, we are unable to effectively impact our community. But this is a political rant for another book. For now, we'll focus on our distinct lack of privacy and what to do about it.

As of now, there are nearly 8 billion people on this planet and nearly 400 million in the US alone. The world sends over 200 billion emails per day[3]. 3.2 billion people, a third of the world's population, are online[4]. Nearly every person on Earth has a cell phone[5]., and nearly half the US has a computer as well[6]. About 8.3 trillion SMS messages are sent annually[7]. That's a lot of data flying over the ether.

These numbers represent a huge challenge to the agencies that would listen in. It is not inconceivable that they have the resources and ability to do it, though. I've watched over the years as the latest and greatest supercomputers from IBM have been sent to the US Department of Energy for nuclear simulations. The question is, what happens to last year's model? And that very question may be moot if "terrorist activity" warrants public acceptance of covert surveillance.

My issue with these privacy sacrifices is that they weren't necessary 250 years ago, why are they necessary now? Surely we were capable of horrific acts then - when the very notion of rights was conceived - why should we be so careful to abridge them now?

---

3   http://www.radicati.com/wp/wp-content/uploads/2014/01/Email-Statistics-
    Report-2014-2018-Executive-Summary.pdf
4   http://www.itu.int/en/ITU-D/Statistics/Pages/facts/default.aspx
5   http://www.itu.int/en/ITU-D/Statistics/Documents/facts/ICTFactsFigures2014-
    e.pdf
6   http://www.ctia.org/your-wireless-life/how-wireless-works/annual-wireless-
    industry-survey
7   http://www.portioresearch.com/en/blog/2013/17-incredible-facts-about-mobile-
    messaging-that-you-should-know.aspx

Chapter 2: Privacy

Again, these are signs that the government is beyond our control, and the last vestige of power we have, our vote, is also being leeched. I am a patriot, make no mistake, for the republic that the US is intended to be.

So we must proceed under the assumption of a deficit of privacy, that every action is recorded, and that it will inevitably be used against us should the US government find it worth their time. And that's what it's all about, staying under the radar, being trivial enough to avoid case escalation. These clandestine agencies will, at the end of the day, need human eyes to evaluate the "red flags" popping up. We must randomize and obfuscate to keep those eyes occupied with nonsense, and a little misdirection wouldn't hurt.

Since public hotspots are used by so many people, it makes them perfect for obfuscation. Being among a group of fellow surfers makes it difficult to identify you specifically. They also expose your business to those next to you, but there're ways to address that using a VPN at a minimum. You must also be careful to avoid man-in-the-middle (MITM) attacks which are commonly setup in these public areas.

VPN's are discussed in Chapter 8: Virtual Private Networking (VPN) and are recommended as a minimum for Internet connectivity. This will obscure and protect, reducing your footprint. Changing your computer's traceable information, i.e. MAC address,

14

HDD SN, window size, and IP will also mix it up. Again, even if you're totally benign today, tomorrow may be a different story. Practice safe computing.

Your Internet provider will change your IP upon request. Your telephone carrier will also change your phone number. Banks will change account numbers (discussed in Chapter 23: Bank Drops). Do not be afraid to request changes in your physical identifiers, as this may have no effect upon a concerted attack but *may* help make the evidence inadmissible (should it become an issue).

TOR, I2P, and other Darknet interfaces not only protect your privacy, but they also keep the government busy. As more people implement these tools, the more difficult spying becomes for covert agencies. You can rest assured it's the focus of their efforts right now. Cryptography, in general, keeps those supercomputers working at maximum power, and that's the type of misdirection that wouldn't be required if our rights were adequately preserved.

The object of the game here is to keep yourself from endangering yourself now or in the future and to help protect the community around you from illegal intrusion. I want *everyone* to have privacy and protection, not just those that have read this book. Whistleblowers like Edward Snowden have revealed what's really going on behind the scenes, but his public expatriation may impede similar revelations in the future.

Chapter 2: Privacy

3: TCP/IP Basics

The Internet Protocol (IP) is a method of digital communication. There are other forms, but only IP is used on the Internet. It was designed to link together distant networks, "inter"-"net" communication. This protocol has evolved over the decades and is the basis of the Internet.

The Transmission Control Protocol (TCP) is one of the several means of moving information across the Internet and is by far the most commonly used. Its main benefit is reliability. TCP uses connections to transport files between computers over the Internet.

Packets are fixed sized chunks of data transmitted over the Internet. Files are chopped into packet-sized pieces and sent to a recipient. They are re-assembled into useful files or instructions at the receiving side. Web pages, pictures, text, movies, audio, all is sent via these packets.

Each packet contains information about the sender and recipient, called a connection. This information is used to distribute and properly reassemble the files. Each party is defined by both a MAC address and an IP address. The MAC[8] is intended to be a permanent identifier of your computer. The IP address is assigned and intermittently changed based on your MAC address.

Routers are located throughout the Internet and are responsible for steering information towards the intended recipient. These routers may log packet movement, showing who's sending what to who and when.

When you connect to a website, a TCP connection is established, and your computer requests the default web page (if none is specified). The server received your request and responds with a banquet of information. This information is interpreted by your browser and presented for your browsing enjoyment.

Secure Socket Layer (SSL) connections encrypt the data going back and forth when possible (you connect using HTTPS). This prevents prying eyes from EASILY reading or altering your packets. This is better than nothing but still insufficient should an

---

8   see Chapter 5: MAC Spoofing

agency get involved.

TCP/IP is meant for honest people to easily and efficiently share data and files. Security was an afterthought, and in the grand scheme of technology, it was rightfully so. We didn't invent guns to massacre school kids, or the Internet to steal money.

Chapter 3: TCP/IP Basics

4:   <u>**Shady Connections**</u>

If you want the utmost privacy, security, and safety, you'll want to implement some healthy habits. Diligence may save your ass. Don't be sloppy, and exercise extreme caution when being naughty.

First, never connect to the Internet at home unless you're capable of leading separate lives. If you access something from home, then drive up to Starbucks to hack the CIA, they will note your inactivity at home. Evidence is not your friend, and sometimes something MISSING is evidence. Like being questioned by the police, give them NOTHING. Circumstantial evidence will still get unwanted attention.

The ideal connection cannot be traced back to you in any

way. Surveillance video can be damaging. Your MAC and other hardware identifiers can rat you out. Login information and web-based logins can obviously screw you over. Even the proximity to your home is a factor. There are many ways your activity can be traced. We'll address the key vulnerabilities in the chapters to come.

Most public wi-fi hotspots have surveillance video. Should activity get traced back to that location, it would narrow the list of suspects down substantially. It's just a matter of law enforcement "following the money" to single you out. Then they start building their case, and you just keep plucking along unsuspectingly helping them in their efforts.

Choose a wi-fi hotspot without surveillance, like a hotel parking lot, or wear a simple disguise. Remember, they'll build their case AFTER they know you're doing bad things, so keep moving around. Don't be a typical crook and return to the scene of the crime. Choose a spot on the other side of town, or even another town/state, and finally pull the trigger there.

Video can also capture license plates, so think things through. Taxis only keep a known phone number in their records, and if you're smart, you've already got a burner (anonymous pre-paid) for those purposes. Cabs have backseat video too these days, so avoid using them to pull up to the very curb of the target hotspot.

So now you've arrived anonymously and can't easily be physically identified. Great! Before connecting to the hotspot, you'll want to disguise your computer by changing (or spoofing) your MAC and other PC-specific information. This is explained in the next two chapters.

Chapter 4: Shady Connections

5: __MAC Spoofing__

The Media Access Control (MAC) address is a unique identifier of your computer or smartphone. More specifically, it identifies your network card in a network. It is used in the TCP/IP protocol to route IP packets exclusively to your computer over the Internet. Your MAC ("address" is implied throughout) is sent and shared in certain packets to accomplish this. After someone knows your IP address, your MAC defines you on the network. Forensic examination includes this critical piece of data. It's part of your "fingerprint" on the Internet.

If you're naughty online, your MAC will incriminate you, the "final nail in the coffin". There are a few effective ways around this. Firstly, many newer laptops have a firmware-based MAC that is easily changed. Secondly, Windows allows you to change the MAC within the registry. Lastly, there are programs that will enable quick and easy changes to network settings, including the MAC.

Your MAC might be changeable in the system BIOS. It probably isn't. In older days it was hard-coded, but as the number of network conflicts increased, this practice was deprecated. The address is a group of 6 sets of 2-digit hexadecimal numbers, in the form of "12-34-56-78-9A-BC".

An Organizationally Unique Identifier (OUI) in the MAC identifies them the manufacturer. The OUI is typically right at the front of the address. For example, consider a network adapter with the MAC address "00-14-22-11-A3-4B." The OUI for the manufacture is the first three octets: "00-14-22" (Dell).

MAC filtering is the process of permitting (or excluding) certain MACs on a given network. This is used to more tightly control access but is not a real deterrent to a determined hacker these days. By listening in to network traffic (sniffing the network), you can find permitted MACs.

Wireshark[9] and *NMap*[10] are two popular examples of sniffers that can expose a network's details to your inquiring eyes, making access trivial. Sniffers are an essential part of any hacker's toolkit,

---

9   https://www.wireshark.org/
10 https://nmap.org/

but outside our discussion here.

For the purposes of this book, we are really only interested in hiding, obfuscating, or masking our MAC to avoid leaving fingerprints. The last five octets ("14-22-11-A3-4B" in the example above) are what we need to alter. To accomplish this, you can change the "NetworkAddress" registry value for your network adapter[11] (NIC) in Windows. Remember that the first three octets identify the manufacturer, so changing that sequence to a random number will flag the alteration as such. BE CAREFUL. Windows is picky about the *first* octet, and as a rule **ALWAYS** backup your work. Write it down with pencil and paper, because backing up to a file still leaves a fingerprint. In fact, if law enforcement gets your laptop with an intact hard drive, you're screwed no matter what you do.

After changing the MAC, always reboot. You may use "ipconfig /all" or "netstat -r" in a Windows command window to view your MAC. After you change your MAC and reboot, a public network may request you to re-login. This is an excellent indicator that all is well with the world. You can change your MAC as often as you deem necessary. If the network suddenly becomes inaccessible after changing your MAC, simply revert to your original MAC and retry.

---

11 HKEY_LOCAL_MACHINE\SYSTEM\CurrentControlSet\Control\Class\
{4D36E972-E325-11CE-BFC1-08002BE10318}

Chapter 5: MAC Spoofing

Another method of MAC obfuscation is a specially designed hardware bridge or switch. Some are available on the open market to do just that. You plug in your ethernet connection and connect the other side to a hard-wired network. You can also use an external wireless NIC instead of an integrated one. In many cases this is preferred, albeit a bit conspicuous in Starbuck's. To erase your fingerprint, trash the device thoroughly. Be careful to buy it anonymously, and don't procrastinate on security.

The last topic is software-based MAC spoofing. I'm a big believer in the power of software, but a HUGE skeptic of human nature. Software by its very nature is flawed. Open-source software is more openly and thoroughly scrutinized, but that doesn't mean it's much safer. Having said that, firing up a program and having it change your MAC quick and dirty has a certain appeal.

Technitium[12] or Macshift[13] (amongst others) will enable you to quickly and easily change your MAC on the fly. If a tool is difficult to use, people tend not to use them, so ease in this area may save your ass. Change your MAC routinely, especially before and after logging on to a new network. Protecting your identity, your privacy, and your safety largely hinges upon good habits, and this is one of them.

---

12 http://technitium.com/tmac/index.html
13 http://devices.natetrue.com/macshift/

6: **HDD SN Spoofing**

Your hard disk drive (HDD) has two serial numbers: one is integrated into the firmware on the drive itself, and the other is assigned during formatting. These two numbers can be used to identify your computer on the Internet. PayPal is one of the companies that will check your hard drive serial number when you log on. Spoofing here is more easily and effectively accomplished using software.

The first number, embedded into the hard drive, identifies the drive for warranty purposes. Changing it will void your warranty, and actually writing the number to firmware may be extremely difficult for the layman. This number varies by manufacturer in type and length, and can be viewed using the appropriate HDD checker

Chapter 6: HDD SN Spoofing

written for the manufacturer and available from the same.

The second number is assigned during HDD format and is in the form "ABCD-1234", all hexadecimal numbers. This number identifies the hard drive partition (the volume) to Windows. It does not follow any specific method of assignment and is more-or-less random for purposes of our discussion here.

Windows installations, as well as many other software installs, examines your HDD format SN to verify authenticity. Changing the number on the drive itself may kill Windows. It's easy to change programmatically but highly discouraged. One option is to boot from a disposable USB drive. That will gain you access to the computer and Windows while enabling a panic-based escape route.

While HDD SN's are used to ID your node, it is important that they be the same, or at least expected, by your target. So, for example, to access PayPal you would change your HDD SN to match what it was when you created (or last accessed) your account. Unlike MAC's, you don't want new random numbers popping up for your drive. You also don't want your "known" SN to match the *actual* HDD SN in your computer. So what do you do?

Resort to software like *Pb Downforce*[14] to change your integrated HDD SN or the freeware *Hard Disk Serial Number*

---

14 https://www.raymond.cc/blog/download/did/1092/

Changer[15] to change your volume ID. The major stress point here is that you should reset your SN's to their original values after accomplishing your mission and before rebooting your computer. This is another area of discipline.

Few online sites currently inspect these numbers, but that could change rapidly, and government agencies may already be logging it surreptitiously. There's no way to know. The key factor is that software must be run to extract your SN from your computer, and that is difficult for someone to hide consistently. So for the FBI to watch your activities using this method is impractical, but possible. Web sites that pretend to be secure would probably implement it, though. And they'd get your MAC and other info and tie it all together with a bow and stash it away for future use.

---

15 Search for: www.xboxharddrive.com

Chapter 6: HDD SN Spoofing

7: __Password Protection__

The heart of security lies within password protection. Everything you are is based on the protection you surround yourself with. Tight protection hinges upon using passwords that are difficult to hack, yet easily usable. Password databases are the most effective tool in this regard.

Many people make the grave error of reusing passwords, especially those that they want available on the fly. While this may be appropriate for situations that are inconsequential, for the most part, it's a mistake. We're creatures of habit, and revealing these habits open us up to exploitation. Random difficult passwords are the bane of hackers, and that should be your goal.

The ideal practice is to implement random passwords, using

the highest number of available characters, via a password generator. Password databases, such as KeePass[16], include a password generator that can specify the permissible characters. Every time you setup a new account, create and store a new password in the database. Browsers will happily store these login credentials, and connecting is a snap. For sites such as Pandora, who cares if it's cracked? But if their database is hacked, and your password is stolen, you'll be able to rest assured that your other accounts are still safe.

For other sites, such as banking or Darkweb Markets, you will obviously want to step it up. NEVER save the passwords to sites that affect your money or security. This should be common sense, but the statistics are alarming. 55% of Internet users use the same password for most, or all websites[17]. 80% of us are concerned about online security, and 40% of consumers have had a security incident of some sort, whether it be a stolen password, account hacked, or a notice of same in the past year[18]. This is a sad commentary on our online disciplinary state, but a cornucopia of opportunity for hackers.

If someone wants your passwords, they'll get them with enough perseverance[19]. Malware has been stealing passwords for

---

16 http://keepass.info/
17 https://nakedsecurity.sophos.com/2013/04/23/users-same-password-most-websites/
18 http://www.entrepreneur.com/article/246902
19 https://thehackernews.com/2015/11/password-manager-hacked.html

decades. Social engineering has been around since fire. We can only do so much but making ourselves a difficult target is the best defense. Predators will move on to easier prey. If YOU have to jump through hoops to pull up passwords, a hacker or government agency will have a bit more than that to deal with. Make them earn their pay!

As a hacker, if I were to stumble across an account that was weakly protected, I would explore further knowing I had a good chance of getting another hit. I would examine the strategy of the password design, and extract information from it. Bebop0182 may indicate an important date - "0182". "Bebop"? Is that a pet? Anagram? What IS that? I'll figure it out, and when that phone call comes asking if your password is still "Bebop0182", you'll be sure to update me with the new one. RANDOM passwords protect you from these assaults.

If you MUST use a password that compromises security, then try to adhere to the following tactics:

- Use a passphrase, such as "This is the greatest book ever written in 2016", which would become Titgbewi2016 – it's easy to remember and fairly difficult to hack. Use this type of password for accessing your password database manager. Use movie titles or song lyrics, anything that is stuck in your head. Just don't reuse it ANYWHERE!!

Chapter 7: Password Protection

- Use Leet[20] if you're comfortable with it. *Consistently* replacing an "o" with a zero makes the password much more difficult to figure out, and even makes shoulder surfing harder. In an Internet cafe, it can be difficult to tell when a camera or investigative eyes are watching you, even recording you. You don't have to go all out, just use substitution enough to mix it up and make them earn their pay.

- Use the maximum characters permitted. Combine passphrases and numbers as needed to perturb assailants.

- Check out your physical surroundings and computing environment before keying anything in. Use malware detectors. Keep your back to the wall.

- Change your password every few months. Corporate hacks are much more common than reported, and your password may already be stolen, and you'd never know. Change it occasionally to be sure, before your enemy gets around to using it.

Avoid using online password managers. These may be convenient as hell, but they're equally dangerous. Use a locally run program that maintains an encrypted local database that you can

---

20 https://en.wikipedia.org/wiki/Leet

access offline and hide as needed. This is a higher level of physical security that few people require, but having a backup is never a bad idea either. Online databases are painfully insecure in the grand scheme of things[21]. Once an online site is hacked, ALL the accounts are breached, and the temptation and target is too great a risk for cautious users.

Two-factor authentication ("2FA" - also referred to as two-step verification) is growing in availability and popularity. It incorporates a second method of authentication, such as a text message or predetermined synchronized code, to authorize access and transfers. Your favorite ATM (hopefully) uses 2FA by requiring both an ATM card *and* a PIN. This is discussed more in-depth in Chapter 12: Bitcoin and Cryptocurrency.

If you practice these simple procedures, then your passwords will protect you as much as they can. If you routinely install insecure programs and surf filthy websites, stop reading and just give your money to charity and turn yourself into the police for being a total idiot. Hackers are programmatically testing you more and more at every turn these days. Make it harder for the government, and extreme for hackers. Use different random difficult passwords everywhere.

---

21 http://www.wired.com/2015/06/hack-brief-password-manager-lastpass-got-breached-hard/

Chapter 7: Password Protection

8: **Virtual Private Networking (VPN)**

A virtual private network (VPN) extends a private network across a public network, such as the Internet.[22] That's what Wikipedia will tell, and it's a purely technical and somewhat ambiguous way of describing this security must-have's. Withing the context of this book, a VPN obscures your true IP to a destination website and enhances the security of your Internet connection.

Websites receive identifying information from your computer so that they may reply. This info can then be traced back to the person that pays the bill, and usually, that's you. If you're doing something dirty, then they'll use this information as evidence. Obviously, you want as little evidence as possible.

---

22 en.wikipedia.org/wiki/Virtual_private_network

Chapter 8: Virtual Private Networking (VPN)

VPN functionality is part of TCP/IP communications. That is the language used by the Internet. Windows supports VPN's, and a VPN connection is easily configured within Windows. The requirements are merely a VPN server, a username, and the password attached to it. Once connected, the remote server will typical force another layer of encryption upon your communications. This is good.

Free VPN accounts are available. There are a plethora of choices, but all do the trick. Performance is the main factor. The most popular free VPN's include:

- VPNBook.com releases it's passwords via it's Twitter account[23], and the other settings are posted on the website. Aside from the password, the settings remain constant. You must configure the connection within Windows (or whatever OS you use) manually, then use the Twitter announced biweekly password as needed. Note that VPNBook's privacy policy specifically excludes bad behavior from its protection.

- OpenVPN.net features a self-configuring client called PrivateTunnel[24] that will do the hard part for you.

- Hide.me allows you to setup an account and allows manual configuration as well as automatic.

---

23 https://twitter.com/vpnbook
24 https://www.privatetunnel.com/home

Servers obviously require money to operate. The free servers listed above have only so much they can do for free. Many paid VPN providers will not only offer much greater speed and response; they'll include other features that can be incredibly useful.

The tradeoff is once again anonymity. If you pay with a credit card, this leaves a trail. If you use VPNBook, it's servers are so heavily burdened at times that you might never connect. Many VPN's now accept Bitcoin, but this is not as anonymous as you might think. The less interaction you have with any company, the better chance you have of staying out of court. If you plan on doing nothing bad, now or in the future, then trails are irrelevant.

Once you've selected a VPN, you'll connect to it immediately after connecting to the Internet every time you want the enhanced privacy and security. Your connection speed will be affected, so using it constantly is unwise unless the benefits are regularly required. This is your call, but always err on the side of caution when in doubt. Your every activity online may also be scrutinized down the road, so perhaps constant use is justified.

Assuming you're using broadband, you'll only connect to a VPN as needed to protect your online activities. If performance is unimportant and privacy paramount, leave it on 24x7, but remember that all activity (legal and not-so) will be traceable back to your VPN and ultimately – you - if you leave a haphazard trail. Of course, if

Chapter 8: Virtual Private Networking (VPN)

you're using hot-spots appropriately, then you'll never be in danger from law enforcement. Other agencies can and will track you as they deem necessary.

9: **Socket Secure (SOCKS)**

Socket Secure (SOCKS) is a networking protocol. It can be used over the Internet.

A socket is one end of a connection made between two computers over IP. Packets are typically sent from one socket to another over the Internet, through a channel. *Secure* sockets is an updated and upgraded method of secure communications through these channels.

A SOCKS *server* proxies HTTP securely.

Tor offers a SOCKS server interface to its clients. Other programs that implement SOCKS include PuTTY and WinGate. I2P bypasses the need for SOCKS entirely.

Chapter 9: Socket Secure (SOCKS)

Using the programs mentioned above adds a certain layer of additional privacy and security to your traffic, but in can only really be used by software that incorporates it, and is activated by default. So if it's available, use it. For example, Vuze[25] permits SOCKS connections and when downloading torrents it may be wise to use the SOCKS protocol. You would connect to Tor, then activate Vuze with SOCKS enabled, and you'd have that additional layer of obscurity. Your downloads would be much slower, but only you know your level of paranoia (and it may be appropriate!)

---

25 http://www.vuze.com/

10: <u>**Proxy Servers**</u>

A proxy server forwards HTTP traffic. There are a number of different types. Some are free; many require a subscription. They are most commonly used by large companies to help protect their internal networks. Only a specific type of proxy server protects anonymity. For the purposes of this book, we'll focus on that one type: the *anonymous open proxy server.*

The proxy server is basically a smart router – it directs web packets towards their assigned targets. A user logs in and is assigned an IP address. This IP is then used to represent the user in all forwarded packets. This differs from a VPN because the proxy is usually just web-related. VPN's cover all traffic, including non-web based access. Being connected to a proxy server does not automatically guarantee any level of privacy or obfuscation.

The proper time to connect to a proxy server is after connecting to your VPN. This chains the connection together, making a trace extremely difficult, if at all possible. The proxy server will also become your new geographic location after connecting to it – any websites needing to ensure you're in the US will look for a US IP. If you need an IP from a specific country, you will connect to the appropriate proxy server that serves that country.

The ideal proxy server will have a minimal effect on your connection speed, amounting to little more than another hop during HTTP routing. It is intended as a level of redundancy to simply hide you deeper and increase your security.

Proxy servers are the tool that permits you to be physically located in Russia or China and appear to be in Atlanta, using some poor slob's credit card from nearby. You pay for your VPN; you go cheap on the proxy server. A proxy server can also assign you a static IP. This comes in especially handy when repeatedly accessing secure sites that expect consistency. If you're going to be promiscuous, wrap that rascal with both a high-quality (expensive) VPN and proxy. It's cheaper than a lawyer.

Another layer of physical security can be created by using a DIY hardware proxy server. This involves a simple concept –

connect a repeater at your victim's network, and connect to it wirelessly from a distance. There are a number of ways of doing this, but all involve intruding upon a target network, and that puts you on a map. Dangerous. You want to avoid geo-location whenever possible.

The upside to a remote connection is that in a congested area, you're only narrowed down to a few thousand people. For routine access, this does make you harder to trace. If the FCC gets involved, though, they'll find you in a minute. The whole wireless bridge thing you see on TV is real and easy to do, but these days it's also easy to get caught doing it. Because we're wireless, we think invisible. Not so, my friend. Those signals you're sending are literally on the radar.

For a one-time trigger, yeah I can see it. If you keep the receiver in your home, and happen to notice people in suits perusing your cookies, you can remotely self-destruct your network or data or both. I think you'd be better off with a panic button of sorts, but I digress; for the purposes of this book, a hardware proxy is deprecated. If "they" have located your geographical point of access, you're not being careful or you're being greedy and deserve some alone time to think about that.

Chapter 10: Proxy Servers

11: <u>Cleaning Up</u>

A system cleaner is required to cover your tracks and eliminate evidence of your dark activities. While you CAN do this manually, it is silly to do and dangerous if you slip up and forget something at the wrong time. You know how Mr. Murphy works – the day before they serve the no-knock warrant is when you'll leave something unattended. Automate whatever you can, and vigilantly update and double check the routine. This is where "small and nimble" becomes a virtue.

Amongst the various tidbits of incriminating evidence, be certain to securely erase the following routinely:

- Cookies

Chapter 11: Cleaning Up

- History

- Temp files

Of course, these things shouldn't exist, to begin with, if you're practicing due diligence and discipline. The files listed above, however, may come about as the result of simple research. Any research you do should be stored on your USB stick, the one safely stashed in the fake electrical outlet behind your bedroom door, but the traces it leaves behind should be erased quickly. Give them nothing!

Each browser has its own special method of cleaning up[26]. Should you then go to a command prompt and look around, you might be surprised how much is left behind. As a forensic data recovery specialist, I've been able to retrieve files and information deleted years prior. The file systems used today do not promote privacy. If you save a file, there's a good chance some or all of it is still there for curious eyes to examine.

FAT, FAT32, and the NTFS file systems used by personal computers simply mark sectors as available or not. A sector can hold 4, 8, 16k of data, or more! Many files fit inside a single sector. When you delete a file, or say when your browser deletes a file, the data itself is left intact and the entry is marked as available. That's it. All

---

26 https://kb.iu.edu/d/ahic

those cookies and temp files linger, waiting for the flunky forensic dude to copy the damaging state's evidence to your growing file.

Use a secure deletion program routinely. Military-grade erasure writes to a sector 3 or more consecutive times, each a predefined pattern. This tells you something – erasing something a mere two times is insufficient. There is plenty of documentation that explains how to extract overwritten data. It's not easy or cheap to do, but it is available. A good cleaner will overwrite allegedly unused sectors, making recovery impractical if at all possible. This erasure will take a while, hours or longer depending on the size of your hard drive.

Non-magnetic media, such as USB sticks, do not suffer from such ghosts. Optical media, though, can also be recovered in many cases. If you're saving to CD or DVD, you're really just creating a nice pile of evidence for your imminent jury trial. As a rule of thumb, save to USB stick only. Securely wipe as needed (use 3-ply).

A practical routine I learned long ago is this:

1. Secure erase (or format) USB stick "B"

2. Copy the files from "A" to freshly secured "B"

3. Verify "B" (test it out)

4. Securely erase "A" (yes, a redundant step)

5.   Rinse and repeat next after your next session

This eliminates any orphaned files on the sticks. In the event of a catastrophic emergency, stick the stick in the microwave oven and make popcorn. It won't take more than a few seconds to permanently destroy all the chips and the data contained within. But should you fail to get that far, the only evidence left behind is what you already know about.

Another common misconception is the format procedure. It does not erase the vast majority of data. Formatting, again in the interest of speed, just marks the drive available and does some minor housekeeping. Think how long it takes to copy a gigabyte file. That's how long it takes to write a gigabyte to a hard drive. Multiply that by the number of GB on your hard drive, and that gives you an idea of the time required for a single erasure. A *secure* erasure will require triple that (or more). The length of operation should tell you it's intensity (or the programmer's incompetence).

I like command line tools. They can be used in scripts and generally run faster. Sdelete[27] from Microsoft is one such free tool that also does sector erasure. Eraser[28] is a Windows-based free tool. There are others available from a variety of companies, but the key features to look for is sector erasure and ease of use. People tend to

---

27 https://technet.microsoft.com/en-us/sysinternals/sdelete.aspx
28 http://eraser.heidi.ie/

avoid difficult tasks, and having things single-click increases their use and overall effectiveness. Opponents will debate this, arguing that ease of use encourages complacency. They have a point. Be diligent and re-evaluate your security every few months or more. Attack from the other side and see what you can find to be used against you.

Chapter 11: Cleaning Up

12: **Bitcoin and Cryptocurrency**

Cryptocurrency is a purely digital concept. Unbacked by gold or any form of substance, it's purely virtual, but like any currency, it has worth as long as people value it. Bitcoin is the most popular form of Cryptocurrency today, and is accepted by a growing number of vendors. Cryptocurrency, especially Bitcoin, is the only method of payment accepted or recommended for use on darkweb markets[29]. For purposes of clarity, we'll only refer to Bitcoin in this text.

Bitcoin is a method of payment secured by encryption. Transactions are difficult to trace and therefore largely anonymous. Payments are irreversible, unlike credit cards, PayPal, checks, or even cash.

---

29 See Chapter 18: Darkweb Markets

Chapter 12: Bitcoin and Cryptocurrency

It is decentralized. No country owns it, prints it, or controls it. It is immune to war and national distress. In fact, it usually increases in value during times of crisis (like gold). Aside from buying or selling large quantities (similar to the stock market), no country can influence a Bitcoin's value.

A free "digital wallet" stores your public and private keys required to access your funds, which are stored on a globally shared and publically accessible ledger. These wallets can be online or off for enhanced protection. A transaction occurs by sending a quantity of Bitcoin, represented as a fraction (say .5604 or 1.38221 BTC for example) to an account number sent to you by the recipient. Your wallet will allow you to enter these two numbers and transmit it. Once sent, it is placed in a queue at random ledger's server[30] and awaits cryptographic confirmation. This usually takes upwards of a few minutes, which is determined by the current transaction load of the system.

Confirmation certainty depends upon the vendor comfort level. For all practical purposes, the payment is fairly certain after a single confirmation, but to be sure most vendors require a minimum three confirmations. These confirmations are performed by the same computers that "mine" Bitcoin, a subject outside the scope of this book. Once confirmed, the funds appear in the vendor's own wallet.

---

30 https://blockchain.info/

Bitcoin transactions are publicly exposed on the global ledger, but the wallets themselves are typically anonymous. The ledger is designed and maintained in such a way that forgery and hacking are virtually impossible.

Bitcoin is not yet considered currency in the United States. This may change anytime, but for now, there are no restrictions over who can exchange it. Quantities in excess of $10,000, however still grab attention due to anti-terrorism efforts. Since the wallets can be anonymous, it's difficult to know who owns what, but when you attempt to give someone $10 grand in US dollars for Bitcoin, they may catch flack over it. Money Transmitting Businesses (MTB's) are obliged to KYC – Know Your Customer. They will want proof of identity and residence.

There are ways around this, but it is akin to money laundering and carries a certain risk. International websites and servers have been established to bring buyers and sellers together. Some are browser-based, most are smartphone apps. The browser-based programs all have apps to complement them.

LocalBitcoins.com (LBC) is far and away the biggest of the bunch. With its app Local Trader, it enables fast and easy trades. They do not require any registration aside from an email account, but the people that own Bitcoin may want more than that before they trust you. The higher the risk, the more the seller will charge over cost. Always use escrow unless you're meeting face-to-face.

Escrow services are available online. They charge a tiny fee, which may be billed to the buyer -or- the seller (or split). Essentially, a buyer initiates a purchase on the escrow; the seller sends the BTC to the escrow wallet. The purchaser now has a certain amount of time to submit payment to the seller. If the seller doesn't receive payment, he can demand his BTC back from the escrow service. If the seller DOES receive payment, he releases the BTC to the buyer. If the buyer pays but the seller doesn't send the BTC, the buyer can then demand the BTC from escrow after proving he sent payment. The escrow service arbitrates any arguments, which rarely happens, so it's good to use.

LBC automatically uses escrow for most of its transactions. It's built into their system, so a separate escrow service is unnecessary. This protects the buyer more than the seller, though. Someone selling BTC on LBC is vulnerable to fraudulent payments. To avoid being scammed, sellers will post and adhere to a lengthy list of rules regarding their offer. They will also look at your history, rating, and whether you've been confirmed by LBC. Most will decline to do trades with someone fresh. If you want anonymity, it will come at a high price and extra effort, but might be worth it.

The purchase amount depends obviously upon your need. If BTC is currently $200 per BTC, and you need to send someone

$300, worth of BTC, then you'd need to buy 1.5 BTC. The price of BTC fluctuates about 5% throughout the day. Next week BTC may be priced at $100, or $300 per, who knows? It moves around like a stock. So buy it when you need it, and don't worry too much about the current value. It translates.

If anonymity is critical, then you can use LBC or an array of other matchmakers to meet locally with a seller. This can be (and should be) face-to-face. There have been incidents of robbery and other bad behavior from both BTC buyers and sellers. Be careful. Meet in a well-lit public hotspot during normal business hours. This is the typically safe procedure:

- Choose a seller near you. Read their fine print and consider their price. Prices can vary as much as 20%, but the amount you're purchasing and their distance from you make a big difference.

- Use LBC (or another) to contact a seller. The price per BTC and quantity is usually set at this point. He will charge a premium to take time out of his day to meet you, not to mention gas and other expenses.

- Agree on a time and meeting place (public hotspot). He is doing YOU a service and will want to meet near him. Comply, but use your common sense.

- Meet the seller, give him the cash. A phone number is handy at this point, but you can work around it if necessary. It will feel weird for both of you on the first meet. Communicate. Using BTC for illegal purposes may implicate the seller if you mention your intent. Shut up. If you were to tell ME that you're going to buy drugs using the BTC I'm sending you, I'd never do a trade with you again.

- Wait for confirmation of BTC release, and you're done. Say goodbye and walk away. Leave positive feedback on LBC regarding the transaction unless it goes very wrong.

Once you've established a level of trust with someone, then you may consider doing business *without* the face-to-face. This is much easier and usually, they charge much less. Methods can include:

- depositing cash to the seller's bank account (quickest)
- mailing cash (obviously risky)
- mailing a cashier's check or money order (tracking)
- PayPal, Credit Card, MoneyGram, and many others

The last methods are discouraged by most sellers. They can all be easily reversed and claim no anonymity. PayPal is especially bad about this, and their methods are absolute madness. Making a cash deposit to the seller's bank account is commonly done. Banks may red-flag the seller's account if caught doing so, so don't do this frequently or for large amounts. Some sellers may have bank accounts specifically setup for this method as an MTB. Use escrow if the seller agrees, and you feel it's necessary.

Use two-factor authentication (2FA) whenever available to

safeguard your wallet and transactions. Google Authenticator[31] is a free smartphone app that generates a unique time-sensitive code that should be implemented IN ADDITION to your password to release BTC. It has gained wide acceptance and few (if any) successful thefts have occurred with it in place. It's an extra step, but a worthwhile one. Another "second factor" is a texted code from the concerned website (like LBC), but this is slower and subject to having a properly registered phone active and sitting beside you. You may not want that phone number to be known, or the phone even in your proximity.

The final and most important point to make about Bitcoin is that you shouldn't trust ANYBODY. I hate to be the one to break it to you, but apparently, there's a bunch of crooks out there looking to take advantage of you. Use escrow. Spread your BTC around to multiple wallets to avoid having your eggs in one basket. Use offline ("cold") wallets when possible to prevent a software attack and subsequent heist. Use unique complex passwords on every site as explained in Chapter 7: Password Protection. Just treat your BTC like the currency it is (but the US denies it being).

---

31 play.google.com/store/apps/details?id=com.google.android.apps.authenticator2

Chapter 12: Bitcoin and Cryptocurrency

13: **the Darknet**

The Darknet is so named due to it's obfuscated navigation and hidden services. Servers operating on the Darknet do not advertise, nor seek to be recognized. They are frequently invite-only, and security is mandatory. Encryption is tight, passwords required.

The *Darkweb* is a subset of this Dark**net**, and the two words aren't entirely interchangeable despite common nomenclature. The Darkweb features websites available using Tor. Other services are available on the Darknet besides Tor, though, including secure anonymous email programs, and other emerging protocols such as I2P.

The Darknet, as described in this chapter, encompasses a broad spectrum of hidden websites and services that are mostly obscured to the public. As such, I won't get very specific about its contents, which is covered in later chapters. The main point to take away is that there is a subtle difference between these dark worlds and clarification is in order.

No, there isn't much child pornography as some might claim about darknets – it is frowned upon by even the most nefarious criminals. That allegation is likely a manufactured myth designed to justify the government's attacks, "It's for the *children*!" Rather, there are plenty of books and other copyright infringements. Drugs. ALOT of drugs. There are also backups of leaked government documents, and books that have been banned in some countries, and movies, and music. The operators and users of the Darknet aren't greasy little perverts running around with sticky hands; they are revolutionaries – seeking to protect themselves and others from the corruption of the modern world. They are, in the greatest sense, us.

14:   the Darkweb

So named because it is "unlit" (or unsearchable by automated means), the Darkweb is a Darknet region of the Internet that promotes and frequently mandates enhanced privacy. You can hop around screaming out your name and IP to every computer that would listen, but aside from being annoying, it would be no different than being on the World Wide Web. The Darkweb is a "parallel" web – but with certain features that ENABLE people to be completely anonymous. You do not HAVE to be anonymous, though everybody else on it will be vehemently so.

The vast majority of Americans believe they are being spied upon by government and commercial agents online. Edward Snowden confirmed this is happening within the NSA. We also believe there is very little we can do about it. When the US constitution was created, there was little spying taking place, and yet it was included as a fundamental right in the constitution. It was THAT important to our founding fathers. Oh my, how they must be spinning in their graves. We can no longer assume privacy in our daily activities, no matter what country we live in.

The concept behind the Darkweb was created by the US Defense Advanced Research Projects Agency (DARPA), the same folks that brought you the Internet. It was abandoned (apparently they have something better going on). Meanwhile, TOR and other software have taken up the baton, and usage of the Darkweb continues to explode.

The destination on the Darknet is referred to as a "service." No matter what the site provides, it's a type pf service, and vendors will expose access to their sites using specific "services." Specialized software is required to utilize these services. The field is expanding, but currently, only a few major players provide access to Darknet services.

Tor (The Onion Router) accesses the Darkweb using a modified version of Mozilla Firefox. It is currently synonymous with the Darkweb, used by the vast majority of Darknet vendors. It is *much* more secure and private than the public Internet, but still has vulnerabilities that can be attacked. For now, however, it's the best choice.

I2P (Invisible Internet Project) and its protocols permit you to use any properly configured browser to access it's services. It is designed with security and privacy in mind and fills the gaps that Tor exposes. Sadly, it's still evolving and hasn't gained the momentum that Tor enjoys. Vendors like proven stability, I2P isn't there yet. This is the software to watch, though, as it's pretty solid and will likely emerge the preferred choice for vendors.

SafEmail and other email programs are discussed in Chapter 25: Secure Email. These services enhance your email privacy and security, though they openly admit cooperation with government agencies. Apart from that, your email is rigorously protected from prying eyes.

Pidgin and other securable instant messengers are discussed in Chapter 26: Secure Messaging. Note that off-the-shelf software is rarely secure on its own – it needs to be tightened up and maintained to provide adequate protection. Instant messengers provide much greater security than email, but only at some cost to convenience. In the grand scheme of things, avoid using email and stick to OTR IM.

Finally, Darknet markets are discussed in Chapter 18: Darkweb Markets and describes what to expect when accessing vendor sites. It is *not* designed to be comprehensive but instead

Chapter 14: the Darkweb

orients you with the basic information required to safely interact with vendors if you should decide to do so.

15: <u>Tor (The Onion Router)</u>

Onion routing is used to obscure your identity and ultimately the nature of your business. Three different randomly selected relays route your packets in layers – each one encrypting your information and making it extremely tough to intercept and decode. Logs of your connection are typically discarded immediately after disconnect. The destination website won't exactly know who you are, and you won't really know who *they* are. Each website has a method of proving their authenticity, and *you* have a login name and password to prove *your* identity.

To simplify the concept, imagine you have a letter to send to Lee. You put a coded letter in an envelope within an envelope within an envelope all addressed to different people. You mail it. The first recipient opens the first envelope and sends the contents. The second recipient does the same with the second, and the third finally sends Lee his coded letter, which he decodes. Nobody knows about anybody except their immediate sender or receiver. Lee can't discover your address, and you don't have to know where *he* lives.

User security is very strong with Tor. Since any routing logs would optimistically be in 3 different countries (3 relays), then law enforcement would need to get subpoenas in all three countries to build a case against a user. This prosecution is not only impractical, it is highly improbable, as any information eventually acquired would still require decryption. Offering your services as an international assassin MIGHT, however, get that desired attention, whereas selling cigarettes would probably be reasonably safe. Researching for a book ("Hi!") is perfectly legal, and therefore the security is irrelevant.

People running servers have a slightly greater risk than users. It is paramount that servers protect all connections, otherwise a seized server may reveal the users. The slightest mistake can be catastrophic, as witnessed by Silk Road and their successors[32]. There is a great body of documentation on the Darkweb to describe proper server configuration. It changes regularly, and I'll not get into it here. It is an ongoing effort to protect server security, and many Darkweb

---

32 http://www.wired.com/2014/11/operation-onymous-dark-web-arrests/

forums exist to help in that regard. Simply put, if you want to start a server, then you're going to need much more information than this book will provide.

When installing Tor, try to avoid changing ANYTHING. Allow it to install with its defaults. Do not adjust any settings unless you understand that all you can possibly do is make it less secure. It is automatically tight. Do not enable add-ons or Javascript, whatever you do. These things can be used to compromise your true IP and thus your identity. Leave it AS-IS when possible: crippled, slow, tedious. That is the very nature of care and security, the "beast."

Always use a VPN and Proxy Server (see Chapter 8: Virtual Private Networking (VPN)). Paid services will give you greater speed and certain critical options, neither of those benefits are required for Tor, though. In fact, the unpredictability of the free services makes them ideal for obfuscation. The important point is that you use both if you want the greatest amount of anonymity. See the corresponding sections in this book for more information.

Tor works perfectly from a USB stick. Password managers also can be executed from a USB stick. Careful people will encrypt their USB drive, install Tor and the password manager on it, and only use the drive when using Tor. Physically hide the drive within your home (or someplace similarly safe) when not in use. Locking it in your personal safe makes it easy for law enforcement to find.

Chapter 15: Tor (The Onion Router)

Don't do it. Leaving a shortcut on your desktop (or elsewhere) tells law enforcement to look for a removable drive. Don't do that either. Being sloppy with your "History" and "Recent Documents" also leaves unwanted clues. Don't leave ANY indication you know what Tor is, what it does, or have it installed someplace. Make them work for their paycheck, and keep them engaged. I prefer to be busy, rather than bored, and I believe your adversaries feel the same way.

The perfect password manager not only erases all traces of itself in Windows, but it's also strong and portable. Searching on the Internet will return a decent list of reputable programs, as well as their pros and cons. Since you should use a VPN and Proxy Server before firing up Tor, and they require passwords, a web-based password manager is discouraged. It would also leave a trace in any other browser you use aside from Tor. Use a portable (self-contained – non-installing) version. Make sure it supports AES-256 or better. Cryptography is constantly evolving and it's important to stay current. KeePass is an example of a strong, portable, and easy password manager.

Do NOT use Tor for routine Internet browsing. It will work, but it may reveal your identity to the non-dark websites you visit. Should they decide to share that information, willingly or otherwise, you will be compromised. In fact, don't browse the web or do ANYTHING with your computer online while using Tor. The object of the game is to be anonymous, and if there's ANY possibility of giving up data, it's not worth it. The question isn't whether to be paranoid, but whether you're paranoid ENOUGH. The information you reveal TODAY may not be harmful TODAY, but tomorrow? Who knows?

It is important to point out that while law enforcement is repeatedly mentioned in this area, it is NOT the only concern or rationalization behind using Tor. Advertising corporations are always creating new ways to track your every move and put products in your face. Resistance is NOT futile here folks.

Privacy is a notion that has existed for millennia and has only been truly jeopardized in the past few decades. Society has functioned well with it in-place, and it is valued in the utmost, but will continue to be degraded unless effort is invested into its preservation. The idea that "only people with something to hide value privacy" is as misguided as believing "only thieves lock their doors."

Chapter 15: Tor (The Onion Router)

16: I2P (Invisible Internet Project)

I2P[33] (Invisible Internet Project) spawned in 2003 and is an anonymizing network that focuses on secure internal connections between users. I2P seeks to create its own internet, unlike Tor that builds upon and adds to the existing Internet. Special software (which is freely available online) is needed to communicate with other I2P users.

The I2P protocol focuses on secure and high-anonymity messaging, including email and IRC (Internet Relay Chat). It's peer-to-peer, and attacks against users are difficult. Censorship and state monitoring are nearly impossible. It's biggest issue is scalability – and its future is uncertain yet promising.

---

33 https://geti2p.net/en/docs

Chapter 16: I2P (Invisible Internet Project)

I2P does not have many of Tor's weaknesses, nor its strengths, unfortunately. Tor has already developed a large user base - and the software plugins that come with it. I2P will eventually gain these things (while having the solid security footing Tor doesn't) but in the interim using I2P shows up on the state radar because it doesn't have many users. This will change as more people adopt the concept.

Tor is unencrypted at the exit node; that is, the data sent to a server is exposed during the final hop. The data being sent to you from the server is likewise exposed. This brief exposure permits those that control the exit nodes to eavesdrop, and many speculate that a good deal of exit nodes are already in the hands of government or corporate entities. This will eventually lead to trouble[34]. I2P does not suffer from this weakness, and that alone may be its future.

Installing I2P programs are as simple as any other, but it will rely upon the existing I2P protocol being in place on your computer[35]. Torrenting, email, and IRC clients are included in the install packages. Your current browser will need to be configured[36] to use I2P, and I'd recommend using a portable version of Mozilla Firefox[37] loaded on our favorite physically secure USB stick.

---

34 https://www.eff.org/torchallenge/faq.html
35 https://geti2p.net/en/download
36 https://geti2p.net/en/about/browser-config
37 http://portableapps.com/apps/internet/firefox_portable

The whole system is very similar to an interconnected series of VPN's, so obviously, you won't need one when you use it, nor SOCKS or even a proxy. In this regard, it's unsuitable for use in fraudulent activity but very useful for acquiring the information needed to begin.

The Freenet (next chapter) is considered a competitor to I2P, but it is felt by many to be more difficult to use and less useful for secure communication and Darkweb hosting. It has limited developer support, and thus restricted growth.

Once I2P is setup, your online experience will be completely encrypted from end to end, although as mentioned previously - the fields are somewhat barren at this point. This will all change rapidly in the next few years, meanwhile, I2P is ultimately the safest communication method in public use today.

Chapter 16: I2P (Invisible Internet Project)

17: **Freenet**

The Freenet[38] is considered I2P's competition, and is also based on a peer-to-peer highly anonymizing protocol..Packets are encrypted end-to-end. It focuses on eliminating censorship and the freedom to express ideas openly. In some ways, it is better than I2P but hasn't gained the level of enthusiasm or support that I2P enjoys.

Freenet solicits users to provide nominal hard drive space on user's computers to make way for a "data store". Files are encrypted and pieces stored in this space, to enable distributed sharing while protecting the user from legal attack. You can't and shouldn't know what is stored in that area. Everything on the Freenet is stored this way, and this is it's greatest strength.

---

38 https://freenetproject.org/

Chapter 17: Freenet

The Freenet is useful, as is Tor and I2P, for gathering and sharing information anonymously. This information can then be used for whatever purposes you see fit.

18: **Darkweb Markets**

Current illicit sales on the Darkweb is estimated to be under $200 million annually as of publication. That number is still growing steadily, but the explosion has ended. The number of "public" markets online also continues to grow steadily, and the number of private markets (invitation only) can only be guessed at, but must also be vigorously expanding.

Most vendors have sold under $1000 in illicit goods, and only 2% have sold more than $100k. A street dealer selling $500/day would have about $180k/year in sales - to give you an idea of the marketplace. Despite the seemingly small amounts of trafficking, it is a HUGE concern to law enforcement due to it's potential.

One estimate holds that over 90% of illicit transactions reach their customers, with the remaining 10% being seized or lost. Some vendors claim even higher success depending upon the method of shipment and the countries involved. Of course, it depends upon the item being shipped as well. A sheet of LSD would have a higher probability of delivery than say, a pound of skunk-weed. A customer receiving a package should NOT open it immediately, leaving it untouched (safely inside your home) for a day or longer. The presumption here is that if law enforcement comes knocking on your door an hour later, you can claim ignorance of the contents and announce your "prior decision" to return it to the shipper.

Most vendors will not ship to PO boxes or anyplace that seems fishy. A refused package will not be reshipped. There exist "drops" that can be used locally for receiving deliveries and then hand-delivering them to you, but I see little merit in that. Of course, separating yourself from the delivery is a good idea, but be careful who you trust. Your ass is likely going to be given up by your buddy when he's given a choice between prison or turning state's evidence. Putting your buddy in jeopardy to begin with probably isn't a nice thing to do anyhow, but maybe he's got it coming? Your call.

Communications between vendor and customer use PGP extensively. Almost all vendors publish their PGP key on their market page. That key is used in ALL communication with the vendor, using the comm program they specify. This can include IRC, email, and in-market chatter. Encrypt everything. Save only what you must. Everything you have on your computer WILL be used against you in a courtroom if it's accessible. Prosecutors will try to coerce you into revealing your passwords if they can't bypass it using their own sophisticated tools. They are good at what they do – you must be better, not only today but in anticipation of tomorrow.

You should routinely change your identity, setting up new accounts under those identities. Notoriety is your nemesis. NEVER use the same identity on two markets unless you are a vendor, and even then the practice is dangerous. While your customers may feel more comfortable with a recognized ID, you will gather more attention and simply become a larger target for law enforcement. Good luck with that.

NEVER use your real name anywhere for any reason. Don't put your initials in the username, or your DOB, ZIP/area code, ANYTHING that can suggest your true identity. "e4Xby2oM" is an example of a UID that is meaningless. The trick is to remember that UID and password combination. There are freely available password managers that will help in this regard, but remember that they save this information and it MAY end up being used as evidence. For this

Chapter 18: Darkweb Markets

reason, many people use USB sticks loaded with Tor and all relevant files associated with it (see chapter 11: Cleaning Up).

19: **Identity Theft**

In 1998 Congress passed the ITADA[39] to address the growth of identity theft.

Due to the crackdown on terrorism in the US, most states have enhanced (under Federal insistence) their requirements for issuing identification. They've also enhanced the security measures used in those ID's. The government is under the impression that terrorists cannot circumvent these measures, and that they'll play by the rules.

Locks only keep out honest people. A person that wants to get in, will. A terrorist or other person of malicious intent can and will easily get a fake ID. They should not be presented to law LEO's

---

39 www.ftc.gov/node/119459

of course, but rest assured that any layman will accept it. Rent a home, a PO Box, or cash checks at will. Over time, as long as you're careful to avoid generating reportable credit, the persona will become yours. Unfortunately, everybody is making copies of everything these days, so your assumption of this identity may eventually be tracked back to your smiling face on the illegal ID.

Forged birth certificates are easy to find on the Darknet, and forged proof of residency is simple to print. Forged social security cards are also fairly simple to produce or purchase, and SSN's are readily available for purchase. Using these, get prepaid credit cards. Then apply for a state ID using these documents. If someone is capable and willing to self-destruct, then they're certainly capable and willing to acquire illicit yet genuine identification. I question the true intent of these anti-terrorism measures, as they most definitely have little impact on actual terrorists' ability to get credentials.

In Chris Rock's book "The Baby Harvest"[40], he discusses the ease with which a person can enter the Electronic Death Registration System (EDRS) in the US and "kill" people off. This digital death requires an act of Congress to reverse- once you're dead, it's over. You can't vote, get a license, do business, pay taxes (or owe them), or even be prosecuted for any crimes. If you're in jail, you can't be

---

40 https://www.amazon.com/Baby-Harvest-terrorist-criminal-laundering/dp/1515014576

tried. You're dead! They've got to release you. The point is that we're barely anything more than a digital imprint these days- and opportunity exists for those that can (and will) alter them.

Shelf babies, creating new virtual people using forged (or hacked) doctor's credentials on the EDRS is an inevitable future for organized crime. These digital babies will eventually grow into virtual adults, and their imprints will be sold as a commodity to those with the cash to become them. The new person can kill off the old, collect the insurance, or take out loans that are forgiven upon death. There's gold in them thar hills! Meanwhile, until these "babies" mature, we must rely on conventional tactics.

In 2014 the Identity Theft Resource Center recorded data breaches at 783 businesses banks etc, exposing north of 85 million sensitive records including SSN numbers. How many more happen without acknowledgment? As the US moves it's focus to cyber-terrorism and tightening up loose borders, much more is becoming vulnerable due to age and the growing sophistication of hackers. The software for low-interest targets remains antiquated and increasingly vulnerable as time moves on.

The feds have delayed full implementation of REAL ID for years, but the Department of Homeland Security is now pressuring remaining states into compliance. This will force an extra layer of confirmation onto identity cards, but it won't affect a truly

Chapter 19: Identity Theft

determined criminal, let alone a state-sponsored terrorist. It's merely
a smoke-screen, a method (like the TSA) to make us feel
comfortable with our nation's security. The truth is, we have very
little actual security, and really have very little need for it. Identity
theft and fraud are going to be a fact of life (and cost of doing
business) for a long time to come.

20: **Credit Card Fraud**

Credit card fraud requires little or no effort to commit. Using your spouse's credit or debit card at the pump or grocery store suffices as a crime. The Darknet marketplaces have multitudes of vendors selling credit card data, as well as identities. This information is easily purchased anonymously, and goods or transfers exacted with little difficulty. Successful credit card fraud is simply a matter of will.

Most people use debit cards. Few people use credit cards when given a choice. This is an error, as debit card fraud is much harder to reverse or correct by the victim. Use your credit option whenever possible, the banks are much more lenient, and the protection is superior. Unless you are carding, you'll want to stick to credit only.

Carding is the process of copying credit/debit cards to blanks. Encoders (magnetic stripe writers) are easily purchased online. Blank cards can also be purchased everywhere from eBay to Amazon. Encoding is accomplished by using a software program to write the stolen information to a blank card. Once encoded, the card can be used at any ATM or another swipe device. For credit cards, you must also know the actual owner's ZIP code. Debit cards require the PIN.

Skimmers[41] are frequently installed at gas pumps and ATM's. These illegal devices are modeled to look exactly like the real thing. They accept your card exactly as expected. Once your card is read and your PIN is stolen, the device will announce it is broken or unavailable, and your info will be rapidly (even instantly) broadcast to the perpetrator. You're screwed. On the receiving end, your data will be posted for immediate sale at a Darknet marketplace, and within minutes cash withdrawals can be initiated.

RF chips are being embedded into some cards these days. These chips essentially broadcast the same information as the magstripe, and this information can be collected without you even removing the card from your pocket. This info is then encoded onto a blank card or used for online purchases. No matter what type of

---

41 http://www.komando.com/tips/278304/how-to-spot-credit-card-skimmers/all

security is used, people are lazy and vendors will cater to it. Your 16 digit code, CSV, and expiration date are enough for a transaction in most instances.

Anyhow, the process of credit card fraud involves merely buying the fullz (card and identity info) on any of the myriad number of Darknet sites and purchasing something of moderate value online. You must then have the object sent to a drop address or arrange a refund to another untraceable card. This is not as simple as it may seem and is, in fact, the most difficult part.

A drop address may be an unoccupied home nearby, a hotel at which you have registered fictitiously, or even one of the many addresses advertised online on the Darknet. The latter charges a fee to forward the product to you, assuming, of course, they're legit in the first place. Part of the battle is convincing the merchant to ship to an address different from the credit card. Many won't. This is where having the victim's identity is useful; you can verify the information to the merchant's satisfaction.

Once you receive something at the door, leave it unopened for 24 hours. If the feds come-a-knocking you can hand it to them and say, "Yeah, I dunno WHAT this is about. I was gonna return it. <insert cheesy smile>" If they're gonna come, it will be pretty quick, usually right behind the delivery driver. Keep your cool. Lawyer up after handing it back. They are NOT your friends, they can, will, and do lie, and are trained to do so. They're just doing they're job – to arrest you. Give them NOTHING (except the package back)!

Keeping the dollar amount low is important. You may be tempted to order a $2000 TV or a brick of gold. Anything over $300 will typically raise red flags, though $500 is the limit for some merchants and credit card providers. Don't be greedy. Stealing $300 per day is nearly $100k per year. The FBI has a minimum threshold before they begin an investigation, and Internet fraud crossing state lines is their jurisdiction. Generally, the limit is $50k, but in some areas, it's as high as $250k. Triggering the FBI is bad, in case you weren't aware, but the optimistic viewpoint is that they only prosecute a small percentage of their investigations. The IC3[42] reports that less than 15% of victims report it to law enforcement, and less than 10% of those are prosecuted. So, you have about 1% chance of being prosecuted for each transgression.

One angle to explore is to use the credit card to deposit money into a gambling site or other type of exchange, then transfer the money from that account into another account you can cash out. I won't name particular sites here, but any site that permits you to deposit funds using a credit card is potentially useful. Once the money is deposited, and the hold is released, you withdraw. Bitcoin is another useful currency in this regard. Purchasing BTC using a

---

42 https://www.ic3.gov

stolen credit card is a common scam these days, and once the BTC is transferred to your wallet, it's irreversible.

Another tactic is using prepaid debit cards that you can load online. Again, once the money is loaded and released, you withdraw at the corner ATM. Just be aware that state and local law enforcement may come knocking on your door someday if they recognize the ATM picture you posed for. It doesn't matter how many hops the money makes, it will eventually be traced to you if you use an ATM. Virtual currency like Bitcoin is much safer in this regard, as you can securely and privately sell it and get cash in hand without much trepidation.

There are vast numbers of ways to use a stolen credit card for personal gain; it's just a matter of thinking it through. In most cases it won't come back to haunt you UNLESS it's a card from your state, in which cases your local LEO's will eagerly get involved. Of course, buying gas using a local card is much easier than an out-of-state one. Local purchases with a local card (in general) are easier but much riskier. Use common sense here.

Credit card fraud is on the rise and here to stay for now. Credit card companies make exorbitant amounts off of their consumers[43] with some estimates as high as 25% of Internet commerce! Figure the merchant is charged about 2% for every

---

43 http://www.creditcards.com/credit-card-news/bank-yields-loans-1276.php

transaction, then the consumer is charged a median 12% on balances, so the profits range from 2% up. The amount lost to credit card fraud (from a 2009 report[44]) was $190 billion annually for all types of purchases. While a significant amount, it's just a drop in their bucket if they're taking merely 2% of the $25 TRILLION of the 2016 worldwide eCommerce projection[45]. Online sales alone for the US is projected to be $327 billion in 2016. The point is that while fraud hurts, the credit card companies aren't going broke.

Merchants bear the brunt of their sloppiness, and an annual loss of 1% is the normal cost of doing business. Your theft will cost someone something. Should you choose to do it, be prepared to pay the price and buy some friends while you're on the outside, but if you're careful, it's easily accomplished.

---

44 http://www.forbes.com/sites/haydnshaughnessy/2011/03/24/solving-the-190-billion-annual-fraud-scam-more-on-jumio/#4df0b68a7db4
45 http://www.emarketer.com/Article/Retail-Sales-Worldwide-Will-Top-22-Trillion-This-Year/1011765

21: __PAYPAL__

PayPal is ubiquitous, but in my opinion, shady. I say this because they inexplicably shut down my legitimate account with neither explanation or appeal. I did nothing wrong, but apparently their security policies in place decided I violated some obscure rule and killed my 10-year old account. 45 days later I was granted access to my money. They have serious customer satisfaction issues, so I feel no remorse in berating their business practices and printing less than positive feedback.

If you do any amount of research, you'll find that PayPal will limit or suspend your account for trivial and unaccountable reasons. They're constantly defending against new lawsuits, and as of this printing, have been forced to improve their "attitude". Now that I've vented, I'll share the myriad ways to avoid the limitations that some people claim are inevitable. They are overly careful to avoid charge-backs and ultimately make a profit; this I understand, so work with them to use them.

A PayPal account is useful for moving small amounts of money around as well as paying on many online sites. If you don't have an account with them, I don't know what to say. Setting one up is pretty straightforward, and they will request all sorts of verification. They also track a vast array of statistics about your computer to quickly ascertain your identity when logging on.

They look at your IP, your time zone, the language selected for your keyboard, and your HDD serial number before verifying your user ID and password. They will red flag you if your provided home address, phone number, or bank accounts were ever used by someone of whom they disapprove. They are unforgiving and will lock up your money should they suspect you ever had anything to do with anyone they don't like, and apparently they can legally do this. Having said that, make sure your computer reports to them what they expect to see when you created the account.

You can change your phone number, your mailing address, and even your bank account numbers if they are red-flagged. You'll have to setup a new account with all fresh identifiers should your account get suspended. They will request your SSN. Lying about it is identity theft, but they won't check it. I've been told they can't check it, but they do have the list of compromised SSN's so don't be sloppy. PayPal is a great deal of effort for minimal reward, but in some cases, it's required.

Don't ever do transactions over $2000, and keep your totals under $4000 monthly. Start slow and over time build the amounts. Established PayPal accounts are available for purchase on the Darknet, as well as compromised ones. Be aware that buying one and changing things around may get it shut down, and that the person you bought it from is a crook. I can't stress the "slow" part of this enough, be patient and setup a few different accounts (if possible) using all different numbers and dedicated proxy servers to keep them active. Given enough time, every account will get suspended. Be careful.

Using a freelancer site, you can sell a "service" to yourself and pay for it with PayPal. This is cheap and appears legit for all intents and purposes. You can also sell items to yourself, and potentially others willing to pay the inflated prices. This is one method of laundering money and is, therefore, illegal and hence I discourage it, but since the FBI is unlikely to get involved it is your call. As stated over and over again, I advise you to obey the law and leave that piece of doo-doo company alone and unmolested.

Chapter 21: PAYPAL

22: <u>Cashing Out</u>

Getting credit card information from the Darknet is a simple matter. For a few dollars (or less) you can get all the required information to purchase many things online. The issue is, how do you do this without getting caught? Certainly, purchasing the items isn't the hard part. Everybody's made online purchases. The items arrive at your door. Great! But with a purchase via a stolen card, the FBI or state authorities might be dressed as the deliveryman. This would obviously make your day difficult. Actually, this would never happen – I exaggerate, but the point is that discretion is important to avoid criminal charges for your criminal acts. You've purchased stolen information, and now you need to commit a crime and get away with it, otherwise why would you have done it. There are many ways available, here are some of the easiest and post popular, but don't assume complete safety in any event.

CC Cashout: purchasing foreign or Cryptocurrency using stolen credit cards online

SAC: Safe, anonymous debit card for the eventual withdrawal. This can be any card that you have control over; that cannot normally be canceled by anyone else. Creating a new identity and buying a prepaid card, then registering it under that identity, is one method of achieving this. You are compounding your fraudulent activity by two offenses this way, though. Obviously, make sure the card cannot be traced back to you, and don't forget to smile for the ATM cameras recording[46] your withdrawals.

Method One: Wallet 1

1) Get a SAC

2) Open an account to launder the money, like Wallet 1 (walletone.com)

3) Get the stolen card info, including birth date and SSN

4) Using the stolen card, load your Wallet 1 account via any

---

46 https://www.fbi.gov/news/stories/2009/november/atm_111609

number of Eastern European exchanges, IE. Russia, Ukraine, etc. (m-obmen.com, moneychange.me, cash4wm.com)

5) To complete the loading, they will need to send an SMS confirmation to a mobile phone from the SAME COUNTRY as the stolen credit card

6) Bypass voice verification with the DOB and SSN

7) Withdraw the illicit deposit from Wallet 1 using the anonymous card at an ATM or wherever

Method Two: BillMyParents.com

1) Obtain two high-quality identities

2) Open an account at BillMyParents.com with stolen identities but a drop address

3) Activate the card when it's received from BillMyParents

4) Add new stolen cards and keep topping up the SAC, use as desired

Another commonly used method[47] is to send the cash either by wire or courier to a group of people known as money mules or smurfers who think they have been recruited to work as receivables clerks or payment processing agents for a legitimate business. But in

---

47 http://www.newsweek.com/2014/03/21/500000000-cyber-heist-247997.html

truth, the job is a fake one and the company fictitious—instead, the mules are just the last step in a money-laundering chain in which they deposit checks in their own accounts, and then wire the money to another bank under your control. For what they believe is the processing of revenue from legitimate transactions, the mules are paid a percentage of the total amount of cash moved.

There are many more methods, but you get the idea.

23: **Bank Drops**

Getting your hard-stolen money deposited in a bank account is the ultimate goal for many but the digital footprints are extremely risky and inherently dangerous. Cashing out in either Bitcoin or cold, hard, paper US dollars is the safest bet. If a bank account must be used, setup a business account.

Personal accounts require government identification and a social security number. Each bank must have a written CIP[48] (Customer Identification Program) to positively identify their customers. Before opening an account, they must verify the customer's name, DOB (for an individual), address, and an identification number of some sort. These policies will vary slightly

---

48 http://www.ffiec.gov/bsa_aml_infobase/pages_manual/olm_011.htm

from bank to bank. They must also perform some level of verification AFTER the account is opened.

A fake ID will suffice if it's high quality. That will also satisfy the date of birth (DOB) and address. The only remaining hurdle is the identification number. Typically a bank will check any supplied SSN to verify ownership. If it doesn't match the ID you've provided, you won't get far. They will check it immediately, either at the branch or online. You're screwed.

An Individual Taxpayer Identification Number (ITIN) is a number given to non-US citizens and even illegal aliens for tax reporting purposes. Form W-7[49] is submitted WITH A RETURN to the IRS and an ITIN is issued within six weeks. The IRS lists the documents accepted, but they must include two proofs, one a government issued picture ID, which can include a foreign voter registration. A birth certificate is an easily produced second document. With an ITIN in hand, you can easily open a personal bank account with the associated identity.

The safest way to open an account is using a business. The bank will require proof of entity; some documentation that verifies the business' legitimacy. They will require your identification as a principal as described above. But after all this is said and done, more transactions of unusual types will be ignored. The account will also

---

49 https://www.irs.gov/pub/irs-pdf/iw7.pdf

charge you monthly fees. After enough time has lapsed, you'll even be able to apply to a clearinghouse to accept credit cards. The US government's scrutiny for account amounts will also diminish as a business. It all depends on how big you want to get.

There once was a time when you could open an offshore numbered account. They no longer exist in that form. While your identity will be protected to varying extents in foreign countries, the US and Interpol will dig in should enough evidence of wrongdoing accumulate. There is no truly foolproof method of storing wealth these days, except for the mason jars full of gold buried in the backyard – and they're too heavy. This is why Bitcoin and Cryptocurrency scares the bejesus out of the government – you can accumulate vast unreported wealth.

No matter which route you pursue, the object of the game is to get money hopped around to your account without it confiscated, reversed, or used against you in court. Setting up an account with a trivial balance, then slowly building the payoff to a crescendo, is the only way to steal significant amounts of cash. A $100 PayPal scam is hardly worth the amount of time and effort involved in creating the identities and opening a bogus account under the scrutiny of suspicious eyes. Go hard or go home – clean them out.

Once your account is opened, you can begin building a history and opening doors that require such accounts. Keep your ducks in a row and the information tight. Don't be hasty, plan things out. We're shooting for that $50k or larger target. Daily transfers over $10k will draw attention, so make sure you have some time to escape with the loot. Setup a Bitcoin brokerage account, and empty your account into it quickly when the money hits. I'm talking home or vehicle loans as the result of identity theft, or insurance payouts. Make sure to grab some of that cold hard cash for your defense fund too.

Another use of national bank accounts is for Bitcoin sales. Using a program such as MyCelium[50] or website like LocalBitcoins.com[51], one can contract to exchange USD for BTC and vice-versa. A deposit is made to the bank account and the appropriate amount of Bitcoin is transferred. Escrows are extremely useful for this purpose, but not necessary if your client is trusted by you. The advantage of this is the relative anonymity and ease of access. It's possible to average a 10% transaction premium, and when moving enough money that can add up.

Some states regulate the process, calling the advertiser a Money Transmitting Business (MTB) which must legally register with the state and comply with those laws. The US federal government has decreed that BTC is NOT a currency and NOT

---

50 https://mycelium.com/mycelium-wallet.html
51 https://localbitcoins.com/

subject to these laws, but that hasn't stopped Florida from attempting prosecution. The results from those cases are still pending, and involved drug sales, so the attack is multifaceted. Florida loves making felons, and will likely become the first state to succeed in attacking Bitcoin trading.

Some banks will freeze your account if they determine MTB activity is occurring. In this event, it's better to have a business account which tolerates a greater variety and location of deposits. It's all about the money – business accounts charge monthly fees, but even if you're paying for a personal account they'll lock up your money if they suspect you're playing with Cryptocurrency exchanges. You're best opening a couple of accounts to keep it safe. Maintain a "main" account about which no one else knows. Have people make deposits into other accounts and do single weekly or monthly transfers (again keep each transfer under the $10k federal threshold).

Accepting cash for Bitcoin legally mandates that you Know Your Customer (KYC). When you apply for an account such as Coinbase[52], they will require certain proof of identity to comply with these international tenets. The goal is to prevent terrorism, but to me, that means anybody outside the box. I find the dentist terrifying, but he's still not classified as a terrorist despite my loud accusations.

---

52 https://www.coinbase.com/

Chapter 23: Bank Drops

These people that do things outside the law need anonymous methods to move large amounts of money. Thus, large brokerages like Coinbase which play nice within the world complies with the rules de-anonymizing BTC transactions. They KYC – know their customer, and unless you want to enjoy a prison stay for some naughty person, you should too if you choose to pursue a career as an MTB.

24: **PGP and Cryptography**

Pretty Good Privacy (PGP) is a computer program developed by Phil Zimmermann in 1991 to increase the security of email and other public communication. Symantec[53] currently owns the company, but the standards are open for peer review, and OpenPGP[54] exposes all. Many people publish their PGP public key – this key enables you to send messages and communicate securely, avoiding incrimination. Encrypted virtual drives may keep you out of prison.

Cryptography is a rapidly evolving field, and older programs should be avoided. Useful programs will be current for about 18 months, perhaps two years. The more unique the method used, the

---

53 https://www.symantec.com/encryption/
54 http://openpgp.org/

more effective it is. Here, a widely-used method makes itself the biggest target, and thus becomes less secure. You also need to come to an agreement with your "partner in crime" regarding the method used. Obviously, this can be tedious, and the tendency is to take the easiest route. Don't. You already know why – GIVE THEM NOTHING!

GNU Privacy Guard[55] (GPG) is the most popular open-source free software based upon PGP. It is command-line operated, designed for Linux, but a Windows-based version is also available[56]. GPG is the cryptography engine replacing the commercially available PGP and is considered to be interchangeable with it.

Your chosen cryptography software (such as PGP or GPG) will create key sets to facilitate secure messaging. The software will also enable you to encrypt files, as well as to encrypt the password required to decrypt them. The more you use cryptography, the more secure you make yourself. Keep your private stuff private – cryptography is your friend (though a bit caustic and suspiciously quiet).

"Public keys" are a certain length, some multiple of 128 characters (1024 bits). Currently, 512 characters (4096 bits) seems to be the gold standard. These public keys are shared with anyone;

---

55 https://www.gnupg.org/
56 https://www.gpg4win.org/index.html

published online, attached to email signatures, etc. and are matched with a partner private key that only you should know.

"Private" keys are just that – private -they are NOT shared with anyone, but they are used to decode/decrypt anything encrypted with it's matching PUBLIC key. The public and private keys are created as a set at the same time by whatever cryptography software you use. New key sets should be treated as passwords and changed as frequently as your paranoia mandates.

Secure messaging and email begins with you sharing your public key. If someone wants to contact you, they encrypt a message or another key with *your* public key, and it is sent back to you. Since you have the private key, you can decrypt what they send you. If you receive their public key, you can encrypt a reply. This explanation is a bit oversimplified, but suffice it to say that communications security via encryption begins with public keys. The rest is immaterial for the novice.

Given enough resources, any encryption can be broken and your secrets revealed. Don't rely upon single layers of encryption to protect you. Avoid becoming a creature of habit – become a creature of chaos. Unpredictability is the hacker's nemesis, and government agencies aren't above employing such people to achieve their immoral yet well-funded goals.

Chapter 24: PGP and Cryptography

USB and other drives can be encrypted, or virtual drives created. Virtual drives are merely large encrypted files, stored on a physical drive, that contain smaller files. Many USB sticks come with security programs that disable unauthorized access. An encrypted virtual drive, created on a secure USB stick, would double-encrypt the contents. The government cannot force you to reveal your passwords[57]. If the cops legally seize your computer, and they find incriminating evidence, you're toast. If it's encrypted, they're stuck trying to decrypt it – and likely that will take longer than the statute of limitations *unless* you're sloppy of course.

Decryption using brute force is made much easier when the contents are known. In previous chapters, I mentioned compartmentalizing information by not posting shortcuts and eliminating browser history. You should delete everything pointing at (or defining) the contents of your files or removable/virtual drives. If you download Tor, delete the download (after installation) too, then empty the Recycle Bin and clear your browser. Leave no traces for anyone to find, because they WILL find something and that's too much.

---

57 https://www.eff.org/issues/know-your-rights#39

25: Secure Email

Typical email is horribly insecure. You can assume that everything in an email is one step away from being public. For doing transactions on the Darknet, all communications must be secured using some form of encryption. Email, by its very nature, is ill-advised. Having said that, there are occasions that mandate it, and my recommendations follow.

Hushmail is the leading Java-based encryption email program implemented in your browser. It has had it's fair share of compromises[58], though, and browser-based email should be assumed to be insecure. I suggest using a separate program to de/encrypt your messages. Yes, it's harder - but more secure - and that's our goal.

Safe-mail[59], after recently being offline for awhile (due to server failures), has returned and like Hushmail offers a browser-based interface. While neither of the above is ideal, they can be useful for sending previously encrypted files using a simple interface.

Neither Hushmail or Safe-mail will go to prison for you. When handed a court order, they will surrender everything and anything they have associated with you. If your emails involve illegal activity and they're unencrypted, you're giving away evidence – provided they know who you are. Connecting to them securely and browsing with Tor avoids identification, but the contents of your email may still be read, so be discreet.

Mozilla' Thunderbird[60] is an offline reader dedicated for email. Enigmail[61] is an add-on to Thunderbird that enables automatic de/encryption using GPG. There are some hoops[62] to jump through in setting it all up, but in the end, this is as secure as email can get. Don't save your messages unless it's unavoidable. Encrypt every message you can to whoever might be able to receive it – this obfuscates your online activity. The problem with this method is that

---

59 https://www.safe-mail.net/
60 https://www.mozilla.org/en-US/thunderbird/
61 https://www.enigmail.net/home/index.php
62 https://ssd.eff.org/en/module/how-use-pgp-windows

your incoming and outgoing eddresses are exposed to prying court orders and keyboards.

There is no perfect solution, except by skipping out all the above and implementing I2P which incorporates it's own secure anonymous email program I2P-Bote. Due to I2P's infancy and I2P-Bote's inability to support legacy email, it is, however, unlike to become mainstream in the immediate future. In the meantime, try to balance anonymity with security. Use Thunderbird where anonymity isn't important, and a web-based server (sending previously and separately encrypted files) when you want your identity secure.

Chapter 25: Secure Email

26: **Secure Messaging**

Secure messaging is an important part of Darknet transactions. Email can only be secured so much; records exist all over, and the email providers admit compliance with court orders. This, of course, makes sense – what company would sacrifice itself for you? Instant messengers, on the other hand, can be relatively secure. Even with a court order in hand, the provider may not be able to supply the requested information to government agencies. With certain IM providers and protocols, the requested historical data just does not exist. *New* exchanges can be intercepted, but there're ways around that.

Jabber is/was a type of instant messenger. It uses the XMPP

protocol to communicate and has become somewhat synonymous with that protocol. New user registration[63] for Jabber has been disabled since 2013, but the protocol itself remains healthy and widespread.

Pidgin[64] is an open source universal IM client and can access most chat networks simultaneously. Pidgin scored seven out of seven points on the Electronic Frontier Foundation's secure messaging scorecard[65] when implemented with the OTR (Off-The-Record) protocol. There are dozens of other clients that implement OTR, but Pidgin is the most popular with Darknet users.

OTR (Off-The-Record) is a cryptographic protocol that provides end-to-end encryption when used properly. When used with an open source IM client, it's very difficult for anyone to intercept your conversation.

When creating an IM identity, use an obscured and secured browser like Tor. This will prevent your identity from being linked to your ID and will help distance you from interception. If "they" don't know who you are, how can they get a court order to monitor conversations that don't apparently hurt anyone? Even if you're totally legit, do it to aggravate them, and they'll focus on someone else.

---

63 http://register.jabber.org/
64 https://pidgin.im/
65 https://www.eff.org/secure-messaging-scorecard

Keeping your IM's secure is a critical part of success while operating in the underworld.

Chapter 26: Secure Messaging

27: **Federal Law and Reality**

The feds only have so much to work with. States are more aggressively pursuing fraud of various types, but the feds are involved when crimes traverse state lines. Most Internet crime is of this nature.

The National Cyber Investigative Joint Task Force (NCIJTF)[66] which is led by the FBI, has deputy directors from the National Security Agency, the Department of Homeland Security, the Central Intelligence Agency, US Secret Service, and US Cyber Command. In cooperation with key corporations from the private sector ("Microsoft exercised its independent civil authorities in this

---

66 https://www.fbi.gov/news/news_blog/botnets-101/fbi-statement-on-botnet-operation

matter'), they are currently focusing on malware creators and botnets.

Botnets are networks of malware-infected computers. These networks can be used for annoying, criminal, or even terrorist purposes. The last being the greatest specific point of interest for the FBI – they want their yard clean. I can understand that. Meanwhile, smaller players are largely ignored at the federal level. Simply put, they don't have the resources to attack the enormous problem at hand. Thankfully, the statistics show that while Internet and identity fraud is still growing, it's explosive growth has mellowed out significantly.

The FBI lags behind, but as their technology and methods improve, their investigations will target more and more people. The NSA is an acknowledged member of the club, so you can be sure the greatest technology running unthinkable software is already on the job, establishing your patterns and correlating your online activity to assign you to some category, which someday may define you as a felon. The larger your radar signature, the more vigorous attention you'll receive.

Attacking banks and other financial institutions may seem like a great way to get a big payout fast, but those organizations will scream (and be heard) by the FBI quickly. Court orders and summons will fly within minutes, and before you can finish your coffee 18 ninjas will rappel out of Blackhawks and serve a no-knock warrant. The US is a bad place to conduct dark business, and most other countries will cooperate completely with US demands. If you're going to target US interests, have a well-planned exit strategy and do so.

The mission of the National White Collar Crime Center (NW3C) is to provide training, investigative support, and research to agencies and entities involved in the prevention, investigation and prosecution of economic and high-tech crime. While NW3C has no investigative authority itself, its job is to help law enforcement agencies better understand and utilize tools to combat economic and high-tech crime. NW3C has other sections within its organization, including Training (in Computer Crime, Financial Crime, and Intelligence Analysis), Research, and Investigative Support Services. Over the last five years, the IC3 received an average of nearly 300,000 complaints per year.

Only an estimated 15 percent of the nation's fraud victims report their crimes to law enforcement[67], while the IC3 estimates less than 10 percent of victims file directly through ww.ic3.gov. The 2014 reported losses of $800 million would then translate to about $5.3 BILLION if all things were kept the same. California, Florida and Texas account for over 27% of complaints in the US (and 35%

---

67 http://www.justice.gov/usao-wdwa/victim-witness/victim-info/financial-fraud

of the losses), and the US files 92% of the worldwide complaints (and 84% of the losses). The FBI only has about 3200 intelligence analysts, and only a fraction are involved in fraud investigations. The FBI's top priorities are domestic security and anti-terrorism.

A white collar crime investigation can easily cost the Bureau (and taxpayers) $200,000 and more, therefore the loss threshold at most FBI offices is $100,000 and a few have a $500,000 loss threshold.[68]

The FBI is not the only agency that prosecutes fraud. The Department of Homeland Security, IRS, US Postal Service, Secret Service, and state and other agencies account for 70% of the assault. The number of prosecutions has slightly declined in the last few years. Identity theft and fraud account for about 27% of the total.[69]

How do you avoid being an easy target for the feds? Avoid repetition and don't leave crumbs. Correlation and timing attacks are obvious clues for them. Don't expose bits of private data with your browsers. Clean up cookies, history, use Tor 100%. White hat hackers know much of what you do. Stay off their radar. Avoid Java/Flash/3rd party apps. The feds will follow the money- hop it around. Never leave your computer open and unattended. Have a self-destruct if needed. Keep your system updated. Use a non-

---

68 http://www.wsj.com/news/articles/SB100014240527023040207045792766523
    95665942
69 http://trac.syr.edu/tracreports/bulletins/white_collar_crime/monthlynov15/fil/

persistent system like Kali. When you have to use a name, choose a common one like Smith or Jefferson- something that's a nightmare to single out. And don't get caught dammit!

Their job to make you believe they're your buddy so you talk. Your job to shut up and get a lawyer. Make you look guilty? If they want you guilty, they'll find a way, talking or no. If they were gonna let you walk, you'd still be walking. The question is how much do they want you. Clam up, you can ONLY make it worse!

Chapter 27: Federal Law and Reality

28: <u>Secure Login Cheat Sheet</u>

1. Verify your physical security

2. Boot from your USB drive

3. Verify your HDD SN

4. Verify your MAC

5. Verify misc – time zone, display, etc

6. Open your PW manager

7. Connect to your ISP

8. Connect to your VPN

9. Connect to your Proxy Server

10. Open Tor

11. Go crazy

Chapter 28: Secure Login Cheat Sheet

29: Fraud Data for 2014

These are the statistics everyone wants to see, but nobody wants to know. Fraud is everywhere. These numbers[70] are from 2014:

12.2 Million people annually in the US become victims of identity fraud. That's only about .4% of the population (or about 1 in 250 people) but when aggregated the numbers become much more severe:

7.5 % of U.S. households reported some type of identity fraud with a substantial:

$5,130 average financial loss per incident. Ouch!

Identity theft is defined as the unauthorized use or attempted misuse of an existing credit card (or another existing account) the

---

70 www.statisticbrain.com/identity-theft-fraud-statistics/

misuse of personal information to open a new account or for another fraudulent purpose, or a combination of these types of misuse.

Identity theft is big business. Financial losses in 2010 of:

$13 Billion has in a mere four years doubled to:

$26 Billion in 2014 with an expected $3 billion increase annually!

64.1% of the reported thefts involve misuse of an _existing_ credit card, and

35% involve an existing bank account.

Most of the victims were married, Asian, and under age 25, though there was little significant difference between the demographics. The victims of identity theft come in all types and sizes. Obviously, the more income the victim has, the more likely they'll become a target, but even households reporting less than $7500 in annual income were impacted:

Household Income
– $7,500 5.3 %
$7,500 – $14,999 4.8 %
$15,000 – $24,999 4.6 %
$25,000 – $34,999 6.0 %
$35,000 – $49,999 6.6 %

$50,000 – $74,999 7.9 %
$75,000 + 12.3 %

The big southern states had the highest incidence rates, likely due to the number of elderly and the tourist trades. Florida typically leads the pack, but in this report, Arizona somehow took the national prize. The highest identity theft complaint rate victims (per 100,000) were found in:

Arizona 149
California 139.1
Florida 133.3
Texas 130.3
Nevada 126.0

Identity theft is made much harder when your personal data is limited to certain and trusted people. Small towns, where everyone knows one another (and are more likely to notice breaches) are much safer than the high-traffic tourist towns. Unsurprisingly, the states with the lowest identity theft complaint rate victims (per 100,000) were, therefore, northern:

South Dakota 33.8
North Dakota 35.7

Iowa 44.9

Montana 46.5

Wyoming 46.9

In 2014, the FBI prosecuted:

633 Corporate Fraud Cases

> include Insider Trading, Kickbacks, Backdating Executive Stock Options, Misuse of Corporate Property, Tax Violations

1639 Securities and Commodities Fraud Cases

> including: Ponzi Schemes, Advanced Fee Fraud, Commodities Fraud, Market Manipulation, Broker Embezzlement, Late-Day Trading.

1783 Mortgage Fraud Schemes:

> Inflated Appraisals, Fictitious/Stolen Identities, Nominee/Straw Buyers, False Loan Application, Fraudulent Loan Documentation, Kickbacks

2605 Health Care Fraud Cases:

> Fraud schemes include: Billing for services not rendered, upcoding of services or items, duplicate claims, unbundling, excessive services, kickbacks.

419 Money Laundering Cases:

The process by which criminals conceal or disguise the proceeds of their crimes or convert those proceeds into goods and services. It allows criminals to infuse their illegal money into the stream of commerce, thus corrupting financial institutions and the money supply, thereby giving criminals unwarranted economic power.

FBI Statement:

The Federal Bureau of Investigation (FBI) investigates matters relating to theft, fraud, or embezzlement occurring within or against the United States and global financial community. These crimes are characterized by deceit, concealment, or violation of trust and are not dependent upon the application or threat of physical force or violence. Such acts are committed by individuals and organizations to obtain personal or business advantage.

A Handful of Bad Examples:

Central District of California. A woman pleaded guilty to federal charges of using a stolen Social Security number to obtain thousands of dollars in credit and then filing for bankruptcy in the name of her victim. More recently, a man was indicted, pleaded guilty to federal charges and was sentenced to 27 months' imprisonment for obtaining private bank account information about an insurance company's policyholders and using that information to deposit $764,000 in counterfeit checks into a bank account he established.

Central District of California. Two of three defendants have pleaded guilty to identity theft, bank fraud, and related charges for their roles in a scheme to open bank accounts with both real and fake identification documents, deposit U.S. Treasury checks that were stolen from the mail, and withdraw funds from those accounts.

Middle District of Florida. A defendant has been indicted on bank fraud charges for obtaining names, addresses, and Social Security numbers from a Web site and using those data to apply for a series of car loans over the Internet.

Southern District of Florida. A woman was indicted and pleaded guilty to federal charges involving her obtaining a fraudulent driver's license in the name of the victim, using the license to withdraw more than $13,000 from the victim's bank account, and obtaining five department store credit cards in the victim's name and charging approximately $4,000 on those cards.

District of Kansas. A defendant pleaded guilty to conspiracy, odometer fraud, and mail fraud for operating an odometer "rollback" scheme on used cars. The defendant used false and assumed identities, including the identities of deceased persons, to obtain false identification documents and fraudulent car titles.

About the Author

Chuck is a network security consultant living in Orlando, FL.

Involved in electronics and programming since 1978, his nearly four decades of experience started with a microcomputer boasting a 6502 microprocessor. After saving up $500 working in his father's TV repair shop, he embarked upon his digital adventures with a brand new OSI Model 500 – at age 12.

He learned how to program through reverse engineering and the documentation for the chipset. Binary and machine code became a second language, and soon BASIC. Years later, courses at a community college expanded his knowledge to include PASCAL, which (in the Delphi implementation) became his language of choice for the next few decades.

Drawn to technology, he founded a chain of computer repair stores and began creating computer utilities to assist those ends. This culminated in the paradigm shattering "Silent Sword" anti-malware program, and the security expertise that lends credibility to this book.

Everything contained within this book has been hard earned through difficult (and frequently tedious) trial and error. Most credit should be given to the Darkweb community that is all-too-eager (and justifiably so) to boast of their accomplishments.